LIGHT(EN) UP THE WORLD

A Humorous Presentation for Christmas

by Geoffrey Rudd

MOORLEY'S Print & Publishing

© Copyright 2007

British Library Cataloguing in Publication Data.
A catalogue record for this book is available
from the British Library.

ISBN 978 086071 606 8

MOORLEY'S Print & Publishing
23 Park Rd., Ilkeston, Derbys DE7 5DA
Tel/Fax: (0115) 932 0643

CHARACTERS

Ancients

    Luke – a writer

    Zack – a messenger

    Emperor Augustus – a man for all seasons

    Chancellor Alistairius – the taxman

    Empress Juliana – a rose of summer

    Voice

Moderns

    Joe – a car mechanic

    Marie – his girlfriend

    "King Oliver"   )
    "Duke Ellington") – the "Jazz Grates" Tribute Band
    "Count Basie"   )

    Adam – a sheep farmer

    Abe – his younger brother

    Jake – their workman and erstwhile accountant

    Albert David – Landlord of the Star of David

    Mabel David – The wife

    Mother – Hers!

    Justin   )
    Jessica   ) their children
    William   )

    Gertrude Entwhistle   )
    Humphrey Entwhistle) – discerning guests

SETTINGS

A MEETING PLACE Prologue – neutral (empty stage)

AT THE ROYAL COURT Scene One – Emperor's Palace

ON THE WAY (TO BETHLEHEM) Scenes 2, 3 & 4 countryside with views of hills

AT THE HOTEL Scenes 5, 6, 7 & 8 – public room (stage right door leads to/from the David family quarters; stage left door leads to guest rooms)

WHERE IT'S ALL HAPPENING The hotel at night:
Scenes 9 & 10 – outside hotel (stage right door to form main entrance)
Scene 11 – Mr/Mrs David's bedroom

SEEING THE LIGHT Later the same night: in store room at hotel

A MEETING PLACE Scene 14 – neutral (empty stage or use empty store room)

3

SOUND EFFECTS etc

Pre-performance music

Generally – linking music is useful between scene changes. Short extracts of carols and Christmas music could be played or alternatively traditional jazz could be used, particularly in the scenes that herald the arrivals and departures of the jazz band.

Scene 7   Exit All – sounds of jazz band

Scene 8   After Albert says **"Jolly good"** - more sounds of jazz band

Scene 11   After Albert says **"It's certainly bright; it must be the moon"** – Hallelujah Chorus - Messiah (Handel)

Scene 12   After Mabel says **"What is it dear?"** – 'heavenly' music such as extract from Pie Jesu – Requiem (Rutter)

Scene 13   After Abe says **"…you can hear the music"** – extract from Hallelujah Chorus
After Humphrey says **"…deafened by that infernal band"** – repeat extract from Hallelujah Chorus

Post-performance music

FURNITURE AND PROPERTIES LIST

PROLOGUE
Personal: **Luke**: Large folder (Gospel folio)
                Zack: sheet of paper (message)

SCENE ONE
On stage: Potted plant
                Small table with fruit basket
Personal: **Alistair**: sheet of paper (budget book)

SCENE TWO
Personal: **Joe**: spanner

SCENE THREE
On stage: Instruments (e.g. trombone/clarinet)
Personal: **Oliver:** map

SCENE FOUR - None

SCENE FIVE
On stage: Small table, bookings list
Personal: **Mabel**: mobile phone
                William: sheet of paper (bill)

SCENE SIX
On stage: Small table, cloth, cutlery
Personal: **Mother**: feather duster

4

SCENE SEVEN
On stage: Instruments
Personal: **Basie**: Chelsea football scarf

SCENE EIGHT
On stage: Small table, mug

SCENE NINE
Personal: **Joe**: Travel bag, torch
Marie: shoulder bag
Albert: lantern

SCENE TEN
Personal: **Albert**: lantern, night attire
Shepherds: rattles or squeakers

SCENE ELEVEN
On stage: Bed (e.g. two small tables with Mabel sitting up on them, back against wall and covered by a rug
Personal: **Mabel**: night-gown, cap

SCENE TWELVE
On stage: Baby, crib, blanket, and plain furnishings such as table, water jug, table, cardboard boxes, bags

SCENE THIRTEEN
On stage: Table
Personal: **Mabel:** mobile phone
Albert: mobile phone

SCENE FOURTEEN
Personal: **Luke**: large folder (Gospel folio)

LIGHTING

Cue 1   Lighting - general – overhead spots
Prologue
To open Interior (day time) lighting
Cue 2   After **Luke** exits – fade to black out

Scene 1
To open Bright interior lighting
Cue 3   After all exit – put house lights up; stage stays lit
Song 1
Cue 4   At end of song, house lights down; fade to black out

Scene 2
To open Bright exterior lighting
Cue 5   After **Joe/Marie** exit, fade to blackout

Scene 3
To open Bright exterior lighting
Cue 6   After **Oliver** exits, fade to blackout

Scene 4
To open Bright exterior lighting

Cue 7	After **all** exit, house lights up; stage stays lit
Song 2	
Cue 8	At end on song, house lights down; stage fade to black out

Scene 5
To open Interior (day time) lighting; after family exits – stage stays lit
Scene 6
To open Remain on interior (day time) lighting

Scene 7
| To open | Remain on interior (day time) lighting |
| Cue 9 | After all exit, (sounds of jazz band), fade to black out |

Scene 8
To open	Interior (night time) lighting
Cue 10	After **Albert** exits – house lights up; stage to bright general lighting
Song 3	
Cue 11	At end of song, house lights down; fade to black out

Scene 9
| To open | Exterior (night time) lighting |
| | After **Albert/ Joe/Marie** exit – remain lit |

Scene 10
| **Scene 10** | Remain on exterior (night time) lighting |
| Cue 12 | After **Jake** exits, fade to black out |

Scene 11
To open	Interior night time lighting
Cue 13	After **Albert** says "….in the morning they'll have to go", white spot (centre stage)
Cue 14	After **Albert/Mabel** exit, spot off, <u>fade to blackout</u>; house lights up, stage to bright general lighting
Song 4	
Cue 15	At end of song, house lights down, fade to black out

Scene 12
| To open | Interior (night time) lighting; white spot (centre stage) |
| Cue 6 | After **Albert** exits – remain lit |

Scene 13
To open	Remain on interior (night time) lighting, with white spot
Cue 17	At scene end **(Mabel/Albert/ Humphrey/Gertrude** fall to knees), allow pause (5 seconds), then house lights up, but stage lighting stays as "glow"
Song 5	
Cue 18	At end of song, house lights down, stage fade to black out

Scene 14
To open	Bright (interior) lighting
Cue 19	Scene (and play) ends with **(Fear not…..a Saviour, which is Christ the Lord"),** then house lights up.
Song 6	

PROLOGUE

Enter Luke

Luke   Ladies and gentlemen, girls and boys – Welcome to our little play "Light(en) up the World". My name is Luke and I was once a reporter for Channel Good News Television. The story that is about to unfold before you is loosely based on a small book I wrote, many years ago. We take you first of all to Jerusalem.

Exit Luke

Enter Zack

Zack   What ho my dears… Peace be with you… Do you know I've just had the most awful shock. This DHL bloke came up to me and said "I've got a message from God. Your Missus, Lizzie is going to have a baby". So I says to this chap, he was called Gabby actually, funny name for a bloke, "You're having me on – I've been Vicar here for fifteen years, I'm meant to be running a family ministry and there's still just the two of us". And he said "No kid, it's true, God rang up this morning and asked for one of the couriers to take you this message". Here it is – To Zack A. Ria, *[aside to audience]* get it?…the Rabbi at the Central Synagogue. Well you could have struck me dumb. You see the poor girl's getting on a bit and quite frankly we gave up the child idea long ago. I bought a shed instead. And now the Missus is telling me we've got to call him John. Goodness knows why. Mind you, you think we've got problems; that young cousin of hers, Marie – she's also expecting. That fellow of hers, Joe I think it is, he's really getting it in the neck especially from Marie's family.

Exit Zack

Enter Luke

Luke   But now to Rome.

Exit Luke

SCENE 1 – ALL THE BEST PLANS

Enter Emperor

Emperor   Alistair…Alistair…where are you?

Enter Alistair

Alistair   Here I am, Gordon. I was working on my budget.

Emperor   I should hope so, you're meant to be Chancellor of the Exchequer. And stop calling me Gordon, it's Emperor now and in any case I was never Gordon anyway. I told you months ago, the name is August – because our surname is Calendar. *[Aside to the audience]* - Get it?
Anyway, what wheezes have you dreamt up this time? Your idea to set up a compulsory accident insurance scheme for people who play short mat bowling didn't go down too well. We've had hundreds of players outside the Palace. Every time I go out I keep falling over their wretched bowls. And what about that idea to levy a tax on Ministers who preach long sermons? We've had Vicars galore ringing me up to complain. They go on for ages and always have three points to make.

Alistair   Oh no, Emperor. You'll really like this one. What I suggest we do is introduce a residence tax. If we make everyone go back to where they came from, we could count how many people there are from each place and make them pay a poll tax to help pay for all the services that we provide there.

Emperor   What services had you in mind?

Alistair   I don't know but there must be something. We could provide clean streets, employ more policemen, make the buses run on time...

Emperor   You mean we don't do that now?

Enter Julie

Julie   Hello August, have you seen the children?

Emperor – Julie [*pronounced July*] my darling, which ones?

Julie   Why, April, May and June of course…are you going to tell me you've got others.

Emperor   No once we came to September I went off the idea. My dear I want to know what you think of Alistair's latest scheme for raising more money. He wants to make everyone travel to the place where they were born and then pay a special tax when they get there.

Julie   Won't they moan? Why on earth would they want to go?

Alistair   Oh Empress, it could be as a thank you for their happy childhood.

Julie	And I suppose you're going to tell me next that you'll levy a charge for when they travel, to pay for the roads to be repaired because of all the people using them.
Alistair	That's a good idea – we could call it a Congestion Charge.
Emperor	Ooh, it'll be so cool. You never know, it may even catch on as well.

Exit all

Suggested Song Christmas Praise (see page 22)
Tune: Mull of Kintyre by McCartney-Laine)

SCENE TWO – GOING NOWHERE FAST
[Scene – By the roadside]

Enter Joe and Marie

Joe	OK, OK, I know it's not the most reliable car but I'll get it going soon.
Marie	Why you can't get something newer I do not know; I mean a 1989 Fiat Panda. Honestly a donkey would do it faster. And you won't even join the AA.
Joe	It always gets us there.
Marie	Yeah, usually in time to go home again. Anyway, how much further is this Bethlehem? It's already 4 o'clock.
Joe	Only five miles. We'll be there by 5 o'clock.
Marie	And another thing; we've still got to find a room for tonight. You wouldn't listen to me and book. I'm awfully tired and the baby has been moving around quite a lot.
Joe	Don't worry dear, I've been told there are plenty of places.

Exit Joe and Marie

SCENE THREE – BLOWING IN FROM THE EAST

Enter King Oliver, Duke Ellington, Count Basie

Oliver   Come along you two, we've been here long enough. It's time we were on our way.

Ellington   Tell me King, whereabouts did you say this star was?

Oliver   According to my satellite navigational system, he's near a town called Bethlehem in a country called Judea. I've booked us into the International Hotel there. The owner said that it was fit for a King.

Basie   And who exactly is this star and why is he so special?

Oliver   My dear Count Basie, a girl at my court said that according to some magazine called Bliss, he's quite young and is apparently all the rage in those parts. Now come along everyone, let's get this show back on the road.

Ellington   I say Count, are you finding it hard to keep up in your caravanette? *[Basie looks irritated].* You want to try a Freelander like mine for your next battle-wagon.

Basie   There's nothing wrong with it. It's not essential to have an electronic stability programme, adaptive forward lighting or cornering brake control.

Ellington   Yes, but it helps to have a heater that blows hot air, doors that open and be able to get it past 55 in top.

Oliver   Stop going on. Now tell me, how are you two getting on with your drivers. Are they any good?

Basie   Now I have to say that mine, <u>Tom Bone</u> can be pretty noisy at times. When he's at full throttle, his voice is loud enough for a crowd of over seventy. Just think of it, seventy-six Tom Bones all talking at once.

Ellington   Well, I wouldn't say that my fellow <u>Max O'Phone</u> is quite as bad but I admit that he can be a bit cheeky. Like the other day when I asked him to turn off sharp uphill along an A road. And what did he do? – he carried on along the valley which was the B road. I shouted to him – A sharp, not B flat! And do you know he had the sauce to tell me that it didn't matter either way, they both went to the same place.

Oliver   Hmm, that sounds par for the course. I thought first of all that my <u>Larry Nett</u> was a sensible soul. He was a bit shy at first, rather like a Stranger on the Shore, but lately he's started to moan more and more on this trip. He was whinging on this morning about it being a daft enterprise and he didn't like being in the middle of the desert, miles from anywhere and on our way to watch the latest star. He should know that King Oliver *[pointing to himself]* just lives for his music. It comes first for me. It's what life is all about.

Basie	*[Aside to Ellington]* That's true. Once King Oliver gets a new idea he just rushes off without a moment's thought.
Ellington	*[Also as an aside]* Yes, but it only takes one word from the King and you soon fall in behind. That's why you're still only a Count.
Basie	You came along as well.
Ellington	*[Looking to the side]* Yes, quite. Now then, that looks like our two coming back. It's time to carry on with the great expedition. Westward Ho!

Exit Ellington and Basie

Oliver	*[Calling to the side also]* – Ah, there you are Larry. It's time to go, and remember, you may be driving a Shogun 4x4 but I do expect to stay in my seat most of the time. We'll have a little less of the off-road stuff if you don't mind. Now let's roll.

Exit King Oliver

SCENE FOUR - THE HILLS ARE ALIVE

Enter Adam and Jake

Adam	Hey Jake, have you worked out how many sheep there are yet?
Jake	No boss, every time I try, they keep moving.
Adam	It's just not good enough. They're due at market in two days and I need to decide on my price. You'd better get it sorted out by tomorrow.
Jake	Er, boss…
Adam	Yes?
Jake	Remind me again – what comes after 99? *[Adam start to advance on Jake]*

Enter Abe

Abe	Hi bruv, I'm told there's a big festival in town tomorrow night. I quite fancy going. We've been away for so long and I could do with a touch of the bright lights.
Adam	I think I'll pass if you don't mind. I need to do my tax return. You know that wretched man who behaves as though he is an Emperor – the one they call Vetched August Tax.
Jake/Abe	*[together]* - V.A.T.
Abe	Come on, you'll have plenty of time for that. It's gonna be wicked, man, and anyway it doesn't start until late.
Adam	Oh all right, but I must finish that return and get the animals ready beforehand. My work is really important and definitely comes first in my life. You know I haven't got much time for anything else.

Exit all

    Suggested Song Sheep by Roger Jones (from While Shepherds)

SCENE FIVE - MEET THE FAMILY

Enter Mabel [talking on the phone]

Mabel   You want a what…twin en-suite with a nice view? Are you sure you've got the right place? This is the Star of David Inn at Bethlehem. What exactly can you see? Well it's a bit of a hill I suppose, with sheep on it. You could have a side view if you'd prefer. The view there? It's another hill and that's got sheep as well. We don't really go in for sea views here - only hills and sheep. You'll take it; that's very good. Supper is at 6 pm, the lights go out at 9.30 and breakfast is at 7 o'clock sharp. Well, we don't think that's early for breakfast. It suits me to get it over with and most of our guests don't seem to mind. See you on the 24th then. Oh by the way, how did you find us…in Yellow Pages? And the name?.....James – James Nesbit – you're an actor and you do haircuts in your spare time? How interesting.

Ends call

Honestly I don't know what they expect…en-suite bathrooms? I try to make as much money as possible. After all that's what life's all about, isn't it? I'm not spending money on unnecessary things like showers. They'll be wanting television in their bedrooms next. Now where's that husband of mine? Albert!…

Enter Albert

Mabel   Ah, there you are. Tell me that you've finished all the jobs I gave you this morning.

Albert   Oh yes dear, the grate's cleared, the fire's laid and the leaking tap is mended.

Mabel   Wonders will never cease. *[Aside to audience]* – This must be a first, he normally spends his days playing rummikub.

Now do you realise that we're fully booked for the next few days? Are you sure that you've got the rooms ready? And don't forget it's one teabag between two. *[Picks up the bookings list]* This census has brought us good business. Now let's see who's coming. Ah yes there are all these distant cousins from your David family having to register here in Bethlehem and pay their tax. And what's this one?...King… King!!…arriving tonight. Did you take this booking?

Albert   Ah yes, I think I did do that one, he asked if it was fit for royalty; called himself King Oliver. He's taken five rooms for himself and his entourage, as he called them.

Mabel   Why didn't you tell me - royalty here! - oh my goodness. If I'd have known, I'd have raised our prices - a *king*, why that's wonderful. My hair - must get it done. Who can I ask? *[Puts book down and pats hair]*

12

Enter Justin, Jessica and William [carrying bill]

Justin   Hi Mum, I'm starving, what's for tea?

Jessica   The trouble with you is that you never stop eating – you've only just finished that chocolate. *[Pushing and shoving]*

Justin   Hey Dad, the man in room 12 asked us to give you his bill.

Jessica   William, what have you done with it?

William   I've got it here.

Mabel   *[seizing it]* Bill? – What's this for? *[Reads]* For household services… clearing grate, lighting fire, mending leak…*[advancing on Albert]* - you scheming good for nothing…the guests are meant to be paying us not us them.

Albert   I had this important match.

Mabel chases Albert out, followed by Justin, Jessica and William

SCENE SIX - GUESTS ARRIVING

Enter Humphrey and Gertrude Entwhistle

Gertrude   I thought you told me this was a four star hotel. Have you seen the dining room – I ask you, plastic cloths and paper napkins?

Humphrey   I understand it's particularly good value.

Gertrude   Knowing you, you mean cheap. So, how did you hear about it?

Humphrey   It was recommended.

Gertrude   By whom?

Humphrey   By my friend Mr W. W. Webb.

Enter Mother

Mother   'Ello me dearies, don't mind me *[dusts round guests and generally gets in the way]*

Enter Albert

Gertrude   Ah, are you the Manager?

Albert   That's right lady, I'm Albert the Guv'nor

Gertrude   Oh…who was that?

Albert   Her mother. She does a bit of cleaning. OK, Mother-in-law, you can go back to your crochetting*!* *(Say it like that – so it sounds a bit like cricketing)* *[Louder]* I said you can go back to your crochetting!

Mother - *[Starts to exit looking crestfallen]*. All right, all right, I'm not deaf you know. *(Muttering]* But why he thinks I like cricket, I can't imagine.

Exit Mother

Gertrude	Tell me, your hotel, it says Star of David on the front.
Albert	That's 'cos of me, you see, I'm Albert David.
Gertrude	But I thought this was meant to be the Bethlehem International Hotel?
Albert	Well yes, I suppose you could call it that. We do get people from all over the place. There's even a royal party on its way from the Far East.
Gertrude	Really, that sounds good. We do like to be associated with people of influence when we're away. Our holidays are important to us. In fact our lives revolve round our holidays.

Enter Mabel

Mabel	Why, you must be Mr and Mrs Entwhistle. I hope that Albert has told you about the meal times.
Albert	I was just about to, my lovely.
Gertrude	How wide is the choice for dinner?
Albert	*[muttering to himself]* It's toast tonight.
Mabel	There's plenty of choice.
Gertrude	I quite fancy the fish.
Albert	*[still muttering]* Yep – we've got pilchards.
Gertrude	Or again maybe Italian.
Mabel	Pasta perhaps?
Albert	*[aside]* She means spaghetti…on toast.
Mabel	Or even the vegetarian.
Albert	*[chuckling]* Beans will be no problem, as long as they're on toast.
Gertrude	I'll make my mind up later.
Albert	*[shaking his head]* But it'll still be toast.
Mabel	Very well Madam.
Gertrude	Come along Humphrey, I think I'll have a lie down for a while.
Humphrey	Yes dear, whatever you want.

Exit All

SCENE SEVEN – BLOW MAN BLOW

Enter King Oliver, Duke Ellington, Count Basie

Ellington   Did you hear what that hotel woman was saying. She was going on at her poor husband something rotten. Apparently thought that we were royalty and had been bragging to all her friends about us.

Basie   *[Laughing]* Yeah I heard him saying – "How was I supposed to know". Then she went rabbitting on because we turned up late, have brought loads of luggage and have been showing what we can do and thoroughly enjoying ourselves with sparkling non-stop music.

Oliver   Yes, she was certainly laying into him. She's too full of airs and graces if you ask me. After all we aren't just any old band. With names like King Oliver, Duke Ellington and Count Basie, surely people should accept that we are the royal family of jazz.

Ellington   What did you say this place was, an International Hotel? Huh! The only thing that's international about it is the price – twice as much as we normally pay.

Basie   Have you seen the comments book? It's got lots of complaints about the food, the rooms and the service. Do you think they'll moan about us?

Oliver   With music of our quality, not a chance.

Basie   Now King , where's the gig, where's the new star?

Oliver   Just be patient. I've been making enquiries. I believe it's on at some place called the "Shed". It's painted blue and the big event kicks off at three-o-clock tomorrow. *[Suitable scarf displayed]*

Ellington   Anyway, that's for tomorrow – for now, let's get back to our music.

Exit all [Sounds of jazz band]

SCENE EIGHT – READY FOR BED

Enter Mabel and Albert

Mabel   That's nearly it for the day. Have you done your bedtime chores dear – *[Albert mimicking Mabel]* - fed the cat, put the bottles out, locked the doors, warmed my slippers, put the porridge on?

Albert   Oh yes dear.

Mabel   And is Mother in her room?

Albert   Oh yes dear.

Mabel   Well I'm going up.

Albert   Jolly good.

[Sounds of jazz band strike up]

Mabel   Not again. You'll have to ask them to go. It's just too much. Poor Mrs. Jeremiah in room 17; it's brought on her rash again. And as for the embarrassment that you've brought on me. I told everyone that they were royalty; the hairdresser, my beauty consultant and my personal trainer.

Albert   But I didn't <u>say</u> they were royalty.

Mabel   And now I've got a headache. I'll have to go up early.

Albert   There's a surprise. Good night dear.

Exit Mabel

[Albert looking offstage]

Albert   Mother-in Law – what are you doing?… You're looking for your blanket. So where did you leave it, on your chair? Ok it's not there… And no, it's not by the door. Perhaps it's in your room… And you can't find your glasses? They're not on top of your head?… Well it's just that's where you found them last night. Good, is everything all right now? I'm so pleased. Good night… Yes, Mabel has taken one of her tablets and yes, I am looking forward to a good night's sleep.

Exit Albert

Suggested Song Do You Hear What I Hear?
by Noel Regney and Gloria Shane

SCENE NINE – KNOCK, KNOCK, WHO'S THERE?
[Outside the Hotel]

Enter Joe and Marie

Joe Come on, we haven't tried this one. *[Reading the sign]* What's it called, the Star of David Inn.

Marie It looks pretty dingy if you ask me. Just like your Auntie Ada's boarding house in Margate. Still you'd better knock, there can't be many more places. Having to spend last night in the car was too much. I can't have another night like that with me in this condition.

[Joe bangs on the door]

[From inside, Albert's voice is heard]

Albert All right, all right, I'm coming. Goodness knows what time you call this. It's twenty to ten. Mrs D went up ages ago, the lights are out and I'm just finishing my cocoa.

Joe *[calling out]* I say, have you got a room. There's just the two of us – myself and *[Joe coughs]*…….the Missus.

Albert We're full up. Don't you know it's census time. The whole town's full of these Davids.

Joe But I'm a David too – from Nazareth.

Albert Oh my goodness, not another one.

Mabel *[from off stage]* - Who is it, dear?

Albert More people asking for rooms.

Mabel At this time of night?

Albert I've told them we're full. They could be some of your lot, from Nazareth.

Mabel Oh really, well bring them in.

Albert But we're full.

Mabel You never have any difficulty when it's your Jericho crowd and after all business is business.

Albert So what do you suggest?

Mabel What about that store room of yours.

Albert If you insist.

[Albert leads Joe and Marie across stage to "exit" inside the hotel]

17

SCENE TEN – THE BOYS ARE IN TOWN

[Outside Hotel]

Enter Adam, Abe and Jake –[knocking loudly on door – followed by laughter]

Albert   What is it this time – how on earth is a chap meant to get his rest.

Abe   Hey man open up, I'm told that there is a big festival on tonight.

Albert   *[muttering loudly from inside]* – Not more people. You're the fourth lot. Come on, we're closed for the night.

I can assure you that the only thing going on here tonight is that loads of people keep getting me out of bed. What is all this about?

Jake   Easy man. We got it from the Sound of Music message board run by a fella called Gabby. We've been away but it said it was all happening in Bethlehem. A new star was being launched.

Albert   Well it must be somewhere else, now leave me in peace.

Exit Albert [back into hotel]

Adam   Come on you two, bringing me down here for nothing.

Abe   Yeah but now we've come down here let's still try and find this gig. We're here to have fun – it's what keeps me and Jake going. Having a good time is surely what life's all about, right?

Jake   Come on Boss. Me and Abe – we've really been looking forward to this night. And I did finish the counting down.

Adam   Fat lot of use that was. The first time you said there were 47 and then you came up with 86. I had to do it myself in the end.

Abe   And how many were there?

Adam   133.

Abe   So Jake got it right after all – 47 add 86 equals…133.

[Adam chases Abe off]

[Jake exits doing some finger counting]

SCENE ELEVEN - NO SLEEP FOR THE WICKED

[In the middle of the night, in Albert and Mabel's bedroom; Mabel is in bed and Albert is coming back to bed]

Mabel   What on earth is going on? How many times is that you've been up? You really must cut out your bed time cocoa.

Albert   It's nothing to do with that. It's that young couple. The ones you insisted I put in the store. He keeps ringing the bell for things. First it was for more blankets, then it was for more water and this time he wanted a basket. I've no idea what they're up to but in the morning they'll have to go.

Mabel   And what's that shining? Have you left a light on somewhere?

Albert   It's certainly bright; it must be the moon.

[Suddenly the sound of the Hallelujah Chorus strikes up]

Mabel   For goodness sake, what now? If it's that band they can go as well. I'm not having any more of their antics. Come along.

Exit both [with Mabel stomping off and Albert following behind resignedly]

Suggested Song We're Beginning to See the Light (see p 23)

SCENE TWELVE – ACTION STATIONS

[Scene opens with Joe and Marie on stage seated either side of a crib]

Enter Albert and Mabel [ready for a row]

Albert   What on earth…

Mabel   What is it dear?

[They look on to an amazing sight. There in front of them, in their own store room is the young couple Joe and Marie, bending over a new born baby in a basket. There is heavenly music playing and a bright light is shining]

Joe   Now you know why I wanted all those things. Didn't like to say – but thanks for letting us stay the night.

[Albert and Mabel are taken aback and can only mutter – "a baby, a baby"]

[They look towards the shining light. Suddenly a voice booms out – This is my Son in whom I am well pleased – Go into all the world and preach the good news to all people]

Marie   His name is Jesus.

Mabel   *[recovering quickly].* You can't stay here. Albert we must find them a proper room; there are people moving out this morning. Albert will get it ready for you.

Albert   Just wait dear, this is no ordinary baby. Look at that light. Listen to the music. And did you hear that voice? You wanted to have a King here. Well I think you've got one. This is God's promise come true. All the hotel must see him.

Mabel   Yes but not now.

Albert   *[being assertive]* – No, you listen to me for once. You can sort the room and you can do it in the morning. They are quite all right here for the moment but I'm sure that they could do with more food and water, clean clothes and some extra blankets, so see to it ……..now!

Exit Mabel – [looking suitably cowed]

     Meanwhile I am going to tell everyone about this amazing event.

Exit Albert [Joe, Marie and baby remain on stage]

SCENE THIRTEEN - DON'T WAKE THE BABY

[In the Store Room. As the scene starts, Marie and Joe (and the baby), continue on stage]

Enter Kings

Basie   What's going on, what is all this?

Ellington   It's a baby.

Oliver   What time is it?

Ellington   What do you want to know that for, it's the middle of the night.

Basie   Well it's three o'clock if you must know.

Oliver   That's it. That's why we've come here. It's three o'clock – the time for the big event. Behold gentlemen, *[stretches out hand]* your new star -

[Offstage – the voice is heard again – And he shall be called Wonderful, Counsellor, the Prince of Peace]

[Oliver falls to his knees and beckons the others to get down also but they remain standing]

Ellington   But why?

Basie   Yes, why?

Oliver   Have faith, be wise, men. Didn't you hear the music and hear that voice? This God they talk about. He follows his ways, not always ours. And sssh, don't wake the baby.

[The others then get down on their knees in awe too]

Enter Adam, Jake and Abe [If space is limited, suggest the Kings rise and move aside to allow the Shepherds to have the stage]

Adam   I really didn't want to stop out. Are you certain this is it? Surely it's round the back of where we were before.

Jake   Yeah man, sure looks a dump; what sort of gig is this.

Abe   Well I could see a light just now and you can hear the music. *[extract from Hallelujah Chorus]*

Jake   Call that music?

Adam   Listen. *[Offstage the voice announces – Do not be afraid, I bring you good news of great joy, today in the town of David, a Saviour has been born to you!]*

[They too are stunned as they see the store room scene. Abe goes across to the baby first]

Abe   What on earth – [beckoning them in] come and see.

Jake   [not very enthusiastically] - It's a baby.

Adam   [understanding] – listen you two, this is your new star. This is who we've come to see.

[Abe and Jake display wonder and then all three fall to their knees]

Adam   *[continuing]* Sssh – don't wake the baby.

Enter Gertrude and Humphrey [in their night attire] [As they enter Shepherds move aside]

Gertrude   What's going on, why the alarm? That bright light….is there a fire?

Humphrey Yes, it's not really on getting us up in the middle of the night. We had only dropped off from being deafened by that infernal band.

[Another burst of the Hallelujah Chorus]

Gertrude   Oh my… that's not them again, is it?

Humphrey   Hey, just a minute – look over there.
[Advances across stage] My goodness, it's a baby…what's going on, what is all this?

Enter Albert and Mabel [each with phone in hand]

Mabel   *[breaks off her call]* - Sssh…don't wake the baby. They're saying he's going to be very special – some sort of king in fact.

[The voice continues – He is Christ the Lord. This will be a sign for you. You will find a baby wrapped in strips of cloth and lying in a manger]

Albert   *[also with phone in hand]* – George, I've been calling everyone in the hotel, even her Mother, and texting all my friends. Yes I know it's the middle of the night but you must get down here right away and see the baby.

Mabel   *[goes back to her call]* Gloria darling, have you ever known me to get it wrong. That was just a slight misunderstanding about the royal family coming. I assure you that there really is a King here. No I'm not off my beautifully coiffeured head *[pats hair]* and yes I promise that I won't wake you up again at this time, but it's amazing what's happening here at the moment. All sorts of people have turned up. We've got sheep farmers, a jazz band, in fact the whole hotel has got up to see the baby.

Albert   *[still phoning]* – Yes, this child is clearly something special. We don't yet understand fully what it all means but I'm sure that we will before long.

[The voice – Suddenly a great company of the heavenly host appeared with the angel, praising God and saying, "Glory to God in the highest, and on earth peace to men on whom his favour rests."]

[They stop their phoning and with Humphrey and Gertrude fall to their knees]

[After a moment of silence, all the on-lookers exit. Last of all, Marie and Joe exit, carrying the baby, if possible parading him through the centre aisle of the audience]

    Suggested Song Infant Holy, Infant Lowly – in most carol books

SCENE 14 – A LONG TIME AGO

Enter Luke

Luke   Well ladies and gentlemen, girls and boys – we have nearly reached the end of our play, but I wouldn't want to let you go without telling you what happened next. You can find it all in my little book.

The baby that was known as Jesus grew strong both in mind and body and he also was loved by God. For the ordinary people of his day, he was a super star. He helped them when they were sick and told them stories about the meaning of life. Sadly, some of the important people were jealous and thought him a threat to their power. So they plotted against Jesus and had him put to death.

However God had a plan and by the greatest act of all time God brought him back to life. In fact we Christians at [name of Church] believe that he is still living today and that because of the promises of Jesus that you can read about in my book, we can have God with us for all time.

Don't forget that being able to enjoy music, going to work, making money and taking holidays all have their proper place in our lives but they should not take centre stage to the exclusion of our spiritual relationship to God.

So as we enter into this Christmas season, remember again what the shepherds heard.

Voice – Fear not: for behold I bring you good tidings of great joy, which shall be to all people. For unto you is born this day in the city of David a Saviour, which is Christ the Lord.

Suggested Song O Come All Ye Faithful

THE END

<u>CHRISTMAS PRAISE</u>

Chorus: Oh Jesus is King
His name we adore,
His praises we sing
For evermore
Yes, Jesus is King.

V 1   Born in a stable
Under a star
Followed by wise men
Who came from afar;
They entered and praised him
The babe did not stir
As they gave him their gifts
Of Gold, Incense and Myrrh.

Chorus:

V 2 Shepherds too worshipped
The babe in the stall
They had no gifts
But they still heard His call;
Came from the hills
In the dark of the night
To kneel at His feet
What a wonderful sight.

Chorus:

V 3 Though all this happened
A long time ago
Still we remember

How he loves us so.
He died for to save us
From this world of sin
So just open your heart
And let Jesus come in.

Chorus: Oh Jesus is King
Come hear His call,
His praises we sing
He rules over all
Yes, Jesus is King.

© 1978 Geoffrey Rudd

WE'RE BEGINNING TO SEE THE LIGHT

We spend our time counting loads of sheep,
They never stand still; it makes you weep.
We work and work just to earn our keep,
We're beginning to see the light.

Used to work till it got dark,
Swan around the leisure park,
Play the music; what a lark,
Hey, wow! There's a bright light now!

We go away lots of times each year,
We've sailed right around the world, d'you hear,
We've got it all planned out, never fear,
We're beginning to see the light.

Used to work till it got dark,
Swan around the Leisure Park,
Play the music; what a lark,
Hey, wow! There's a bright light now!

We drive them mad ev'ry place we stay,
Our music is what we do all day,
We are the Three Kings of Jazz, OK
We're beginning to see the light.

Yeah!

Words by Geoff Rudd with apologies to Harry James, Duke Ellington, Johnny Hedges
and Don George
© 2005 Geoffrey Rudd

MOORLEYS

We are growing publishers, adding several new titles to our list each year. We also undertake private publications and commissioned works.

Our range includes:-

Books of Verse:
Devotional Poetry
Recitations for Children
Humorous Monologues

Drama
Bible Plays
Sketches
Christmas, Passiontide,
    Easter and Harvest Plays
Demonstrations

Resource Books
Assembly Material
Songs and Musicals
Children's Addresses
Prayers
Worship and Preaching
Books for Speakers

Activity Books
Quizzes
Puzzles
Painting Books

Church Stationery
Notice Books
Cradle Roll Certificates
Presentation Labels

Associated Lists and Imprints
Cliff College Publishing
Nimbus Press
Headway
Social Workers Christian Fellowship

Please send a stamped addressed envelope (C5 approx 9" x 6") for the current catalogue or consult your local Christian Bookshop who will either stock or be able to obtain Moorleys titles.